CROSS

Ten Sketches for Church or Conference, School or College

BY
BOB IRVING

No performance of this play may be given without the written permission of the publisher to whom all applications for performing rights should be made, enclosing a reply paid envelope to the National Christian Education Council.

The performance time is approximately 5 minutes per sketch.

Published by:
National Christian Education Council
Robert Denholm House
Nutfield
Redhill RH1 4HW

Published for:
RADIUS
Christ Church and Upton Chapel
Kennington Road
London SE1 7QP

British Library Cataloguing-in-Publication Data:
Irving, Bob
  Crosstalk
  I. Title
  822.914

ISBN 0-7197-0795-1

A co-operative venture in Christian Drama by NCEC and RADIUS.

Series Editors: Sylvia Read and William Fry

RADIUS is the shortened name of the Religious Drama Society of Great Britain, bringing together amateur and professional actors, writers, and others involved in religion and the performing arts.

RADIUS exists to encourage all drama which throws light on the human condition, especially through a Christian understanding. It aims to help local congregations towards a deeper appreciation of all types of drama, to inform them of opportunities to see work of a high quality, to give the technical advice and assistance needed for a good standard of local productions, and to help them find ways of introducing the lively arts into their worship.

The society runs a unique lending library, organises an annual summer school, holds regular play-writing competitions and publishes its own magazine.

First published 1992
(C) Bob Irving 1992

Typesetting by One and a Half Graphics, Redhill, Surrey
Printed and bound by The Burlington Press, Foxton, Cambridge.

CONTENTS

CROSSTALK
PRODUCTION NOTES

These sketches are based upon the parables of Jesus, which were in their own time sharp contemporary stories in an established tradition. In order to convey the same sense of immediacy, they are now presented in a highly modern style; some based on the work of standup comedians, and others set in a conventional style.

To make their point, they need to be played with pace and polish. They do not require scenery, any props mentioned are almost always optional, and there is no need for a great deal of movement. Nevertheless they will still need plenty of rehearsal to be effective. The actors must be perfect in order to deliver their lines quickly, clearly and with plenty of projection and attack.

The general tone is comic, but it is not necessary or desirable to add farcical business or to affect broad 'character' acting. The performers all represent more or less straight, modern, streetwise observers, seeing the story in contemporary terms and often reacting in the way we all do, though sometimes in a stylised and exaggerated way. In many of the sketches the majority of the lines should be addressed to the audience with only an occasional reaction between the performers.

In acting or directing these sketches, it is vital to listen to their rhythm. You are advised to read the lines over and over until you hear them in your head like a popular tune. Performers frequently finish one another's lines, so it is important to study the punctuation carefully. These are in any case only suggestions. You may of course have better ideas of your own.

THE ELDER BROTHER

A play for four performers of either sex. ONE and TWO enter from the left and right on their first lines. They link arms and come down centre on the next four lines, which can be delivered as a song and dance to the well known tune.

VOICE 1	Hullo!	
VOICE 2	Hullo!	
VOICE 1	It's a funny old world we live in —	
VOICE 2	And it's always the blooming same:	
VOICE 1	It's the rich wot gets the pleasure,	
VOICE 2	And the poor wot gets — into the kingdom.	
VOICE 1	Eh?	*(Looks at TWO in surprise)*

> *Enter THREE and FOUR from left and right, downstage of ONE and TWO, so that they form a rough semi-circle. ONE and TWO watch each of them as they speak, reacting strongly and occasionally making a comment.*

VOICE 3	Here's a story	
VOICE 4	Jesus told.	
VOICE 3	This man	
VOICE 4	Had two sons.	
VOICE 3	Dave . . .	
VOICE 4	. . . and Rupert.	
VOICE 1	Rupert?	*(Impressed)*
VOICE 3	Dave was a typical . . .	
VOICE 4	. . . Teenager	
VOICE 3	Cheeky . . .	
VOICE 2	Typical!	*(Disgusted)*
VOICE 4	. . . To his mum and dad,	
VOICE 1	Typical!	*(Disgusted)*

VOICE 3	Always in trouble . . .	
VOICE 2	Typical!	*(More disgusted)*
VOICE 4	. . . At School.	
VOICE 1	Typical!	*(More disgusted)*
VOICE 3	Long-haired.	
VOICE 2	I believe it!	*(Nodding)*
VOICE 3	Thrown out of discos.	
VOICE 4	Did a lot of under-age drinking	
VOICE 3	In over-age pubs.	
VOICE 1	I believe it!	*(Nodding)*
VOICE 4	Left School.	
VOICE 3	No GCSEs.	
VOICE 4	Dropped out.	
VOICE 3	Ran off − up the smoke.	
VOICE 4	Landed in a squat.	
VOICE 1	Exciting!	*(Fascinated)*
VOICE 3	No heating.	*(Shivering)*
VOICE 2	Er . . .	*(Not so keen)*
VOICE 4	No cooker.	
VOICE 1	Coo!	*(Definitely put off)*
VOICE 3	No bathroom.	
VOICE 2	Urgh!	*(Disgusted)*
VOICE 4	Got into drugs.	
VOICE 3	Pot first.	
VOICE 4	Then the hard stuff.	
VOICE 3	Got so high.	
VOICE 1	That's really low.	*(Deeply disapproving)*
VOICE 2	A dropped out . . .	*(Deeply disapproving)*
VOICE 1	. . . Freaked out . . .	*(More so)*
VOICE 2	. . . Unwashed out	*(More so)*
VOICE 1	Typical . . .	*(And more)*
VOICE 2	. . . Teenager.	*(And more)*
VOICE 1 & 2	I can believe it, I can believe it!	

ONE and TWO go upstage shaking their heads; it is just what they always expected. THREE and FOUR move centre stage and begin again.

VOICE 3	Meanwhile . . . back at the ranch

ONE and TWO, surprised, come down stage on right and left of them.

VOICE 1	Does he mean . . .	
VOICE 2	. . . The highly-desirable, much sought-after, three-bedroomed, centrally heated, double glazed, with fitted security alarm . . .	
VOICE 1	Semi?	
VOICE 4	So . . . back at the ranch,	
VOICE 3	Brother Rupert . . .	
VOICE 4	. . . Was so good.	
VOICE 3	Unbelievable!	
VOICE 4	His parents hardly knew they had him.	
VOICE 3	He worked hard at school.	
VOICE 4	Never even got a detention.	
VOICE 3	Got nine GCSEs.	
VOICE 2	Nice!	*(Impressed)*
VOICE 4	Three A Levels.	
VOICE 1	Oooh!	*(Impressed)*
VOICE 3	Went into the Civil Service	
VOICE 2	Nice!	*(Approving smile)*
VOICE 4	As an executive officer.	
VOICE 1 & 2	Oooh!	*(Dazzled)*
VOICE 3	Never stayed out late.	
VOICE 4	Always home by ten.	
VOICE 3	Or on a very special occasion . . .	
VOICE 4	. . . Ten-fifteen.	*(Sarcastically)*
VOICE 3	Never chased a lot of girls.	
VOICE 4	But went steady.	
VOICE 3	With that nice girl next door.	
VOICE 4	What was she called?	*(To THREE)*
VOICE 3	Can't remember!	*(To FOUR)*

Pause.

VOICE 4	One day, Rupert, coming home from work, as usual.	*(Starting again)*
VOICE 3	Exactly on time, as usual.	
VOICE 4	Having caught the 5.49 train . . .	

7

VOICE 3	. . . The 6.37 Number 18 bus which brought him neatly . . .	
VOICE 4	. . . To the neatest end of terribly neat Acacia Avenue.	
VOICE 3	So he didn't have to walk far if it rained.	
VOICE 2	That's neat.	*(Admiring)*
VOICE 4	Turned the corner . . .	
VOICE 3	. . . Couldn't believe his eyes.	
VOICE 4	There was his house 'DUNROAMIN',	*(To the audience)* *(ONE and TWO gasp in mock amazement)*
VOICE 3	Ablaze with lights.	
VOICE 1 & 2	Unbelievable!	*(Shocked)*
VOICE 4	Cars lining the kerb.	
VOICE 3	Whopping big party going on!	
VOICE 4	In *his* home?	*(Nodding affirmatively)*
VOICE 2	Incredible.	*(Staggered)*

During the next six lines THREE and FOUR hand imaginary food and glasses to ONE and TWO and all mime drinking. ONE and TWO move left, THREE and FOUR right.

VOICE 3	Place *full* of people.	
VOICE 4	People talking.	
VOICE 3	People laughing.	
VOICE 4	People singing.	
VOICE 3	Lots of food,	
VOICE 4	Lots of booze!	*(Merrily)*
VOICE 1	What's going on?	*(Happy but bewildered)*
VOICE 3	Rupert asked.	*(To ONE)*
VOICE 4	What's going on?	*(In the character of RUPERT)*
VOICE 3	No one listens,	*(To audience)*
VOICE 4	What's going on?	*(Louder)*
VOICE 3	Where's my Mummy?	*(In same character)*
VOICE 4	What's going on?	*(With growing anger)*

VOICE 3	Where's Daddy?	*(More so)*
VOICE 4	What's going on?	*(Still more so)*
VOICE 3	Dad appears.	
VOICE 4	What's going on?	*(Ready to burst)*
VOICE 3	Rupert, Rupert! It's unbelievable. It's great. It's fantastic. Dave's *home!* Your brother is back. He's kicked the drugs, and he's come home. It's incredible!	*(As DAD, very excited)*
VOICE 4	I have had a long day at the office. I think I will go upstairs to my room. Is my tea ready?	*(As RUPERT, grimly)* *(Pause)*

Exit THREE right as offended RUPERT, followed by FOUR, as protesting DAD. ONE and TWO move centre, watching them go.

VOICE 2	Would you believe it?
VOICE 1	Life is such a business.

Returning to song and dance routine.

VOICE 2	It's such a blooming shame.	*(Sings)*
VOICE 1	It's the rich wot gets the pleasure.	*(Snatch of song)*
VOICE 2	And . . .	*(Indignantly)*
	What in heaven, is the point of combing your hair and brushing your teeth and saying your prayers every night, and going to Church every Sunday if God goes bananas over some rotten little drop-out who decides to come to his senses?	*(Stops singing and becomes serious)*
VOICE 1	Agreed!	*(To TWO)*

ONE and TWO link arms and walk to left.

VOICE 2	Agreed?	*(Looks back at audience)*

Both exit.

THE PHARISEE AND THE PUBLICAN

This sketch is for two performers of either sex, but it works slightly better if ONE is a woman and TWO is a man.

A mop and broom are set stage right and left, and two hassocks downstage centre. Enter ONE and TWO from right and left, as they speak. They meet centre and address the audience.

VOICE 1	Hullo!	*(To TWO)*
VOICE 2	Hullo!	*(To ONE)*
VOICE 1	Here's a parable,	*(Downstage to audience)*
VOICE 2	That's very odd.	*(Aside to ONE)*
VOICE 1	Once upon a prayer,	
VOICE 2	Two men . . .	
VOICE 1	*Sexist!*	*(Indignant to TWO)*
VOICE 2	Eh?	*(Startled, to ONE)*
VOICE 1	*Sexist!*	*(More indignant)*
VOICE 2	*Oh,* all right, two women . . .	*(To ONE, giving in)*
VOICE 1	That's better!	*(To TWO)*
VOICE 2	*Eh?* Anyway, two women went into a church,	*(Dumbfounded, then to audience)*
VOICE 1	To pray.	*(Both to audience from now on)*
VOICE 2	One was good . . .	
VOICE 1	No argument.	*(Agreeing)*
VOICE 2	. . . Really good.	
VOICE 1	No question!	*(Enthusiastically)*
VOICE 2	A pillar of the church.	
VOICE 1	That didn't need redecorating,	
VOICE 2	But did all the redecorating.	
VOICE 1	And everything else that needed doing.	
VOICE 2	Went to Services . . .	

VOICE 1	Morning *and* evening.	
VOICE 2	. . . Every Sunday.	*(Picks up broom)*
VOICE 1	Cleaned the vestry . . .	*(Picks up mop)*
VOICE 2	. . . Every week.	*(Both busy cleaning)*
VOICE 1	Polished the brass . . .	
VOICE 2	. . . Every week.	
VOICE 1	Sang in the choir . . .	*(Heads close as if singing)*
VOICE 2	. . . Every week.	
VOICE 1	Led the Women's meeting.	*(Use broom and mop as banners)*
VOICE 2	Very strong!	
VOICE 1	Ran coffee mornings . . .	*(They put down the mop and broom)*
VOICE 2	. . . With biscuits and coffee . . .	*(Mimes giving ONE coffee)*
VOICE 1	Urgh! Very weak.	*(Mime drinking it with distaste)*
VOICE 2	. . . For OXFAM, Christian Aid, NSPCC, RSPCA, Cheshire Homes, Barnado's, Cancer Relief, the Leprosy Mission, War on Want,	
VOICE 1	And the cats and dogs home.	
VOICE 2	So what does she pray about?	*(Enquiringly to ONE)*
VOICE 1	She wants to say thank you.	*(To TWO)*
VOICE 2	Thank you?	*(Questioningly to ONE)*
VOICE 1	Yes, thank you to God.	*(To TWO)*
VOICE 2	That's lovely.	*(Charmed)*
VOICE 1	She knelt down . . .	*(Kneels)*
VOICE 2	. . . On the lovely hassock she had embroidered,	*(Kneels beside ONE)*
VOICE 1	Bowed her head,	*(Bows head)*
VOICE 2	Closed her eyes and prayed:-	*(Closes eyes)*
VOICE 1	Thank you, God, for your goodness to me. Thank you that I can serve you in so many wonderful ways in this beautiful church.	*(As if praying)*

VOICE 2	Thank you for leading me in the paths of right living.	*(As if praying)*
VOICE 1	For keeping me on the very straight and narrow.	
VOICE 2	Not like some I could mention!	
VOICE 1	Particularly . . .	
VOICE 2	*Especially*	
VOICE 1	Not like *her*	
VOICE 2	Who's just crept in at the back!	

Both rise and stare at an empty place downstage left.

VOICE 1	Now, her,	*(Explaining to audience)*
VOICE 2	What had just crept in,	*(Ditto)*
VOICE 1	Was by all accounts . . .	*(Confidentially to TWO)*
VOICE 2	. . . Including her own . . .	*(Confidentially to ONE)*
VOICE 1	. . . Truly and truly . . .	
VOICE 2	A proper slag!	*(To audience)*
VOICE 1	A bottom of the heap . . .	*(Increasing contempt)*
VOICE 2	Proper slag!	
VOICE 1	Had four kids.	*(Gossiping)*
VOICE 2	Wasn't it six?	*(Questioningly to ONE)*
VOICE 1	Two were away.	*(To TWO)*
VOICE 2	In care!	*(Knowingly)*
VOICE 1	She was now . . .	*(To audience)*
VOICE 2	. . . Again . . .	*(Wagging finger at audience)*
VOICE 1	. . . A single parent family!	
VOICE 2	The last bloke . . .	
VOICE 1	. . . Having left − for a long holiday in sunny Devon.	
VOICE 2	In Dartmoor!	
VOICE 1	And another not yet crept in.	
VOICE 2	Living in a council house,	*(With increasing indignation)*
VOICE 1	Naturally.	*(Sardonically)*
VOICE 2	On Social Security.	
VOICE 1	Naturally.	*(Sarcastically)*

VOICE 2	Some of which . . .	
VOICE 1	. . . She naturally . . .	
VOICE 2	Spends on fags.	*(Building to climax)*
VOICE 1	Naturally,	
VOICE 2	Bottles of booze . . .	
VOICE 1	Surprise! Surprise!	
VOICE 2	. . . And somehow she always has money for make-up, colour telly *and* a video!	
VOICE 1 & 2	Huh!	

A slight pause. They both look at the empty place again.

VOICE 1	Now there she is at the back of the church.	
VOICE 2	Not far enough back!	
VOICE 1	Hiding behind a pillar.	
VOICE 2	Quite right, too!	
VOICE 1	Hoping no one will see her.	*(Confiding in the audience)*
VOICE 2	No one wants to!	
VOICE 1	Everyone pretends they haven't seen her.	
VOICE 2	But she prays.	
VOICE 1	And she *prays?*	*(Disbelievingly)*
VOICE 2	*She* prays?	*(Shocked)*
VOICE 1	The very idea . . .	
VOICE 2	Bad enough coming to church.	
VOICE 1	Her sort!	
VOICE 2	What a nerve!	
VOICE 1	Bold as brass!	
VOICE 2	*Trying* to pray.	
VOICE 1	She's praying now . . .	
VOICE 2	Let's listen.	*(Suddenly fascinated)*

ONE kneels at the empty place downstage centre and begins to pray in the character of the disreputable woman.

VOICE 1	I'm sorry.	*(As if praying)*
VOICE 2	Huh!	

VOICE 1	I'm really sorry.	

TWO assumes the character of aggressive mum, standing over ONE.

VOICE 2	Don't say you're sorry. Mend your ways, my girl! 'Mend your ways,' that's what my old mum always said. Mend your ways!	
VOICE 1	I'm so sorry!	*(Still praying)*
VOICE 2	Sickening!	*(Walking away from ONE)*
VOICE 1	I'm so desperately sorry!	
VOICE 2	Pathetic!	*(Looking over shoulder at ONE)*

A pause. ONE rises and stands beside TWO. They both address the audience.

VOICE 2	And Jesus said . . .	
VOICE 1	. . . That this woman . . .	
VOICE 2	. . . Went home again . . .	
VOICE 1	. . . More right with God . . .	
VOICE 2	. . . Than the other woman.	
VOICE 1	*More* than the other?	*(Incredulous to TWO)*
VOICE 2	Very odd.	*(To ONE)*
VOICE 1	That's what I said.	
VOICE 2	It makes you think . . .	*(To audience)*
VOICE 1	He always does.	

They look at each other, baffled, and leave together.

THE TALENTS

A sketch for two performers of either sex.

Three golden caskets stand on a table stage centre, with an upright chair on either side. The caskets could be chocolate boxes, covered with gold paper or paint. Enter ONE, closely followed by TWO.

VOICE 1	Once upon a time . . . Jesus said.	*(To audience)*
VOICE 2	Oh dear, look out.	*(Warning audience)*
VOICE 1	This story Jesus told.	*(More firmly this time)*
VOICE 2	Only a story.	*(Aside to audience)*
VOICE 1	But *Jesus* said . . .	*(Very definite)*
VOICE 2	This is going to be difficult.	*(Very cheeky)*
VOICE 1	*Jesus* said	*(Almost shouting)*
VOICE 2	Sorry.	*(With mock apology to ONE)*
VOICE 1	Once upon a time there was this king.	*(Clears throat and starts again)*
VOICE 2	Don't know any kings.	*(Cheekily)*
VOICE 1	All right then, let's change it. This chap . . .	
VOICE 2	This is going to be ordinary, boring and safe	*(Sarcastic, to audience)*
VOICE 1	How about a fairy godmother?	*(To ONE)*
VOICE 2	I like fairy stories; they don't get at you.	*(Conciliatory)*
VOICE 1	So this fairy godmother appears to these three brothers.	*(To TWO)*
VOICE 2	Let's get on with this story, together.	*(Impatiently to ONE)*
VOICE 1	The fairy godmother.	*(To audience)*
VOICE 2	Gave each of the brothers a golden casket.	*(Offering golden casket to ONE)*

VOICE 1	Super, prezzies!	*(Looking at casket)*
VOICE 2	With a special gift inside.	
VOICE 1	Oh, lovely!	*(Takes casket)*
VOICE 2	So Tom . . .	
VOICE 1	Who's he?	*(To TWO)*
VOICE 2	First brother.	*(Aside to ONE)*
	Opened his prezzy.	*(Continuing to audience)*
VOICE 1	Found inside,	*(Opening casket)*
VOICE 2	Title deeds to a plot of land,	
VOICE 1	In an industrial development area.	*(Bringing out paper and reading)*
VOICE 2	Tom jumped up and down for joy,	
VOICE 1	Two point three times.	*(Jumping up and down)*
VOICE 2	Went off to the Development Corporation,	*(Right of table, to audience)*
VOICE 1	Talked them into making loans,	*(Left of table, to audience)*
VOICE 2	After a thorough market survey,	*(As if imparting a secret)*
VOICE 1	Revealed a deep national need,	*(Very seriously)*
VOICE 2	So far unsuspected and unfulfilled,	*(Most important)*
VOICE 1	For square spaghetti,	*(More so)*
VOICE 2	Coloured puce.	*(Building up to a climax)*
VOICE 1	Built a factory.	*(Starts afresh; excitedly)*
VOICE 2	Filled it with machines.	*(More so)*
VOICE 1	Designed to make square spaghetti.	*(And so on)*
VOICE 2	Engaged 823 employees.	
VOICE 1	Two to operate the machines.	
VOICE 2	One to make the tea.	
VOICE 1	And 820 to colour it puce by hand.	*(Reaching climax addressing audience)*
VOICE 2	Two years later.	
VOICE 1	There is Tom.	

VOICE 2	Winner of the Queen's Award to Industry.	*(Waving paper)* *(Climbs on right chair)*
VOICE 1	For creating employment.	
VOICE 2	Satisfying the national need . . .	
VOICE 1	For puce coloured square spaghetti.	*(Waves casket as well)*
VOICE 2	Driving a Porsche and a Rolls.	*(Changes to sitting on chair)*
VOICE 1	Holidaying in Bermuda. (He sits as if on a deck chair)	*(Posh voice)*
VOICE 2	A success! (Stands and points to ONE)	
VOICE 1	Out of his gift of land.	*(Stands)*

Pause.

VOICE 2	But Dick . . .	*(Starting afresh)*
VOICE 1	Who's he?	*(Putting down the first casket)*
VOICE 2	. . . Second brother.	*(To ONE)*
VOICE 1	Opened his casket.	*(Gives second casket to TWO)*
VOICE 2	Found the title deeds . . .	*(Opens casket)*
VOICE 1	. . . To an old house, a maze of rooms	
VOICE 2	In the old city centre, a maze of old streets.	*(Takes out paper)*
VOICE 1	Amazing! Said Dick. Amazed *and* delighted.	*(To audience)*
VOICE 2	Pirouetted prettily − three times!	*(Pirouettes)*
VOICE 1	Chatted cheerily, cheekily, charmingly to his bank manager.	*(Sits left of table)*
VOICE 2	Got himself a loan.	*(Sits right to take loan)*
VOICE 1	Sorted out the house.	*(Jumps up and gets busy)*
VOICE 2	From cobwebby top . . .	*(Jumps up and gestures up)*
VOICE 1	To dusty bottom.	*(Gestures)*
VOICE 2	Put in new doors here.	*(More gestures)*

VOICE 1	Better windows there.	*(And so on)*
VOICE 2	Installed an *amazing* lighting system.	
VOICE 1	Painted the walls.	
VOICE 2	In amazing colours.	
VOICE 1	Made the old place . . .	*(Rushing busily about)*
VOICE 2	. . . Into an amazing art gallery . . .	*(And so on)*
VOICE 1	. . . On floors one and two.	
VOICE 2	With an amazing self-service . . .	
VOICE 1	. . . vegetarian restaurant.	
VOICE 2	Serving amazing curries of nettle and dandelion leaves in the basement.	
VOICE 1	Then put craft shops.	
VOICE 2	Doing leather-work, candle-making, glass-engraving, macrame, pebble-polishing, egg-decorating, weaving, batik, tapestry, and match-stick battleships in every other spare place, nook and cranny.	
VOICE 1	So there is Dick.	*(Down left to audience)*
VOICE 2	Amazed at his good fortune.	*(Down right, waving casket)*
VOICE 1	Driving his Morris Minor.	
VOICE 2	Holidaying in Florence,	
VOICE 1	Or Glastonbury.	
VOICE 1 & 2	Amazing.	

Pause.

VOICE 2	Then there was Herbert.	*(Puts casket on table)*
VOICE 1	Not Tom, Dick and Harry?	*(To TWO)*
VOICE 2	No, Herbert.	*(To ONE)*
VOICE 1	Oh! Right!	*(Affirmatively)*
VOICE 2	That's it, a right Herbert.	
VOICE 1	Opened his prezzy.	
VOICE 2	Found inside . . .	
VOICE 1	. . . National Savings	*(To TWO)*

	Certificates . . .	
VOICE 2	. . . Worth £500.	*(To ONE)*
VOICE 1	Is that all?	*(Disappointed to TWO)*
VOICE 2	That's what Herbert said.	*(To audience)*
VOICE 1	Can't do much with that.	*(To TWO)*
VOICE 2	Herbert said.	*(To audience)*
VOICE 1	It's not enough to buy a car.	*(To TWO)*
VOICE 2	The salesman said.	*(To audience)*
VOICE 1	Nor enough to buy a house.	*(To TWO)*
VOICE 2	The estate agent said.	*(To audience)*
VOICE 1	It's not even enough for a deposit.	*(To TWO)*
VOICE 2	The building society said.	*(To audience)*
VOICE 1	You can't start a business.	*(To TWO)*
VOICE 2	The bank manager said.	*(To audience)*
VOICE 1	It's not fair!	*(To TWO loudly)*
VOICE 2	Herbert said.	*(To audience)*
VOICE 1	It's not fair.	*(To TWO very loudly)*
VOICE 2	Jesus said.	*(To ONE)*
VOICE 1	Eh?	*(Puzzled to TWO)*
VOICE 2	Who said life should be fair?	*(To ONE)*
VOICE 1	*Pardon?*	*(To TWO)*
VOICE 2	Who said life should be fair? If you believe that,	*(To audience)*
VOICE 1 & 2	*You must believe in fairy godmothers!*	

The last line is delivered loudly in chorus. Leave together.

FOLLOWERS OF JESUS

A 'stand-up comic' sketch for two performers with a NARRATOR, who speaks from a lectern. It works best if ONE is a woman and TWO a man.

Two chairs stand side by side upstage centre. NARRATOR stands at the lectern on stage left and begins to read, when ONE and TWO enter form left and right.

NARRATOR	One day, as Jesus was travelling, one man . . .	*(As if reading a lesson)*
VOICE 1	. . . Freddy Fearless, that is,	*(ONE enters with TWO)*
NARRATOR	Said to Jesus, I will follow you wherever you go.	
VOICE 1	Through thick and thin,	*(Clenching fist, downstage left)*
VOICE 2	Wherever, anywhere, everywhere!	*(Spreading arms, downstage right)*
VOICE 1	Come what may . . .	
VOICE 2	. . . Go what may,	*(Pointing ahead)*
VOICE 1	Over hill, over dale,	*(Descriptive wavy gesture)*
VOICE 2	Through deserts or jungles,	*(As if parting thick reeds)*
VOICE 1	Over mountains,	*(Pointing upwards)*
VOICE 2	In sunshine or rain . . .	*(Raise arm to ward off rain)*
VOICE 1	. . . Snow or hail.	*(Both arms over head)*
VOICE 2	Through storms and tempests . . .	*(Bending over)*
VOICE 1	. . . Blizzards and earthquakes.	*(Bending further)*
VOICE 2	Fighting dragons!	*(Gestures as if drawing sword)*
VOICE 1	Overcoming demons . . .	*(Drawing sword)*
VOICE 2	. . . Giants . . .	*(Striking very high)*
VOICE 1	. . . Evil dwarves, goblins,	*(Striking very low)*

VOICE 2	Vampires . . .	*(Whirling round)*
VOICE 1	. . . Witches and warlocks.	*(Fighting in all directions)*
VOICE 2	Encountering endlessly,	*(Holding sword in salutation)*
VOICE 1	Facing fearlessly,	*(Holding sword in salutation)*
VOICE 2	Bishops, dentists, moderators, and archdeacons,	
VOICE 1	Receptionists, double-glazing salesmen,	
VOICE 2	Facing death and destruction!	*(Sheathing sword)*
VOICE 1	Fearless Freddy said, I will follow you always . . .	*(Sheathing sword)*
VOICE 2	.·. . Wherever you are.	*(Side by side, downstage centre)*
NARRATOR	And Jesus said, I have no home; you will find me in cardboard city.	*(As if reading lesson)* *(Suddenly naturalistic)*
VOICE 1 & 2	That's not very exciting. No thanks.	*(To NARRATOR)*
NARRATOR	And as Jesus travelled on, he said to another man, follow me.	
VOICE 1	But Cecil Careful said,	*(To chair left centre)*
VOICE 2	Bearing in mind the immediate political, socio-economic context,	*(To chair right centre)*
VOICE 1	Is this really a viable position to adopt?	*(Both sit)*
VOICE 2	There is a multitude of interpersonal factors on the agenda . . .	*(Brings out papers from brief-case)*
VOICE 1	. . . Which really have to be thoroughly examined and carefully addressed, in the most insightful manner currently available to us, as meaningful participants in the situation as it presents itself at this moment in time.	*(Brings out glasses-case from pocket)*
VOICE 2	You do understand that I do not	*(Wagging finger)*

	make this response in any kind of negative or judgemental mode.	
VOICE 1	I am most truly, deeply conscious of the inherent value of your proposal with its positive life-affirming implications . . .	*(With hand on heart)*
VOICE 2	. . . Which I am genuinely concerned to hear and respond to, in an authentic way, which will enable a true evaluation of my appreciation of the worth of your suggestion.	*(Putting tips of fingers together)*
NARRATOR	And Jesus said, What?	*(Sudden change as before)*
VOICE 1	Meanwhile, Charlie Churchman said.	
VOICE 2	Follow you?	*(Rising)*
VOICE 1	Follow you? Indeed?	*(Rising)*
VOICE 2	Let me just say that I do think that is a most interesting suggestion.	*(To ONE)*
VOICE 1	It is by no means without merit.	*(To TWO)*
VOICE 2	Indeed not.	*(Smiling to ONE)*
VOICE 1	It has indeed much to recommend it.	*(Smiling to TWO)*
VOICE 2	And indeed I do assure you that we shall give it our most earnest consideration.	*(To NARRATOR)*
VOICE 1	We shall consider it very carefully indeed at our next meeting.	*(To NARRATOR)*
VOICE 2	Have no fear that it will be placed upon the Church's agenda.	*(A step downstage)*
VOICE 1	And, indeed, while I would not wish to pre-empt the course of events, or to prejudge the issue,	*(A step downstage)*
VOICE 2	I think we can say quite, quite definitely, that it will, probably, stand a very good chance indeed of being referred to the	*(Another step downstage)*

	appropriate committee for full and sympathetic consideration. Indeed it will.	
VOICE 1	I would dare to go further and say that I have very little doubt that a discussion paper will be prepared for presenting to all the interested parties.	*(Similar step downstage)*
VOICE 2	You see, we do listen.	*(Moving to join ONE)*
VOICE 1	Indeed, we do, indeed we do.	*(Puts arm round TWO's shoulder)*
VOICE 2	Indeed.	*(To ONE)*
VOICE 1	Indeed.	*(To TWO)*
VOICE 2	But as to actually taking action upon your most interesting request . . .	*(Breaking away towards NARRATOR)*
VOICE 1	. . . That while we would love to follow you, indeed we would . . .	*(Following TWO)*
VOICE 2	. . . And please be quite sure that we do most genuinely say that from the bottom of our cassocks . . .	
VOICE 1	. . . It is so difficult to know in fact what can be done.	*(Shrugging and holding out hands)*
VOICE 2	So often it is distressingly apparent that because of all the conflicting demands, it is by no means clear that anything can be done at all . . .	*(Regretfully to ONE)*
VOICE 1	. . . Other than to maintain the status quo.	*(Similarly to TWO)*
VOICE 2	As the hymn puts it so movingly, Nothing changes here.	*(With a sad smile to NARRATOR)*
VOICE 1	Indeed!	*(With a sad smile to NARRATOR)*
NARRATOR	And Jesus fell asleep. And another man said to him . . .	*(In a realistic voice)* *(As if reading the lesson)*
VOICE 1	Happy Harry, this was.	*(Jumps on to left chair)*

VOICE 2	. . . I will follow you, Jesus. Honest I will! I will follow you.	*(Jumps on to right chair)*
VOICE 1	But first I've got to go home and say goodbye to the folks.	*(To NARRATOR)* *(Gets down)*
VOICE 2	They do matter most enormously, as I am sure you will agree.	*(To NARRATOR)*
VOICE 1	Family life is the most important thing.	
VOICE 2	Get the family life right and everything else will follow.	*(To ONE)*
VOICE 1	Without it there's all this vandalism, hooliganism, homelessness, drug addiction and AIDS.	*(To TWO)*
VOICE 2	That's what we're all meant to have, a wife and 2.2 kids.	*(To NARRATOR)*
VOICE 1	Or maybe a husband and 3.2 kids.	*(To NARRATOR)*
VOICE 2	Where's the extra one come from?	*(Getting down from chair, addresses ONE)*
VOICE 1	That's the husband – men are just big kids.	*(To TWO)*
VOICE 2	Family life is *all* about staying at home together.	*(Takes ONE's hand. To NARRATOR)*
VOICE 1	Watching Blue Peter and Neighbours.	*(To NARRATOR)*
VOICE 2	We are commanded to love our Neighbours aren't we?	*(To ONE)*
VOICE 1	Sons and Daughters; Home and Away.	*(To TWO)*
VOICE 2	Attending PTA meetings.	*(And so on)*
VOICE 1	Voting in all the elections . . .	
VOICE 2	. . . To make sure nothing changes.	
VOICE 1	In a nice semi-detached house . . .	
VOICE 2	. . . With a respectable mortgage . . .	*(Link arms)*
VOICE 1	. . . Paid for by a safe, secure job with an index-linked pension.	*(Smiling at TWO)*

VOICE 2	And where the wife stays neatly home, never even dreaming of working for money.	*(Smiling at ONE)*
VOICE 1	And having as little to do as possible with things that are none of our business . . .	
VOICE 2	. . . Like famines, and conservation − apart from the building Society account.	
VOICE 1	Or single parent families.	*(Moving away from TWO)*
VOICE 2	We should be like the Holy Family, Mary and Joseph.	*(To NARRATOR)*
VOICE 1	Incidentally, what did happen to Joseph?	*(To NARRATOR)*
VOICE 2	Don't confuse the issue. We all know about single parent families.	*(To ONE)*
VOICE 1	Respectable people don't trouble themselves with them; or the homeless.	*(To TWO)*

The last phrase is said to the audience as ONE and TWO go off stage right, arm in arm.

NARRATOR	Who have to live like the birds of the air. And Jesus said, No one who puts his hand to the plough and looks back, is fit for service in the kingdom.	*(As they go)*

THE TEMPTATIONS

A sketch for two readers and three performers. The Bible verses for the readers are given, but you may use any translation you wish.

The two READERS are standing at lecterns upstage left and right. ONE, TWO and THREE are sitting on the floor downstage centre, picking up leaflets as they mention various charitable organisations.

READER 1	*(Reads Luke 4.1-3)*	
VOICE 1	Live-Aid, Band-Aid, Christian Aid.	*(Rifling through leaflets)*
VOICE 2	One per cent for World Development.	
VOICE 3	Tear Fund, OXFAM, Save the Children.	
VOICE 2	CAFOD.	
VOICE 3	Catholic fund for Overseas Development to you uncatholic lot.	*(Rising, to others)*
VOICE 1	Bazaars, jumble sales; sponsored walks, runs, swims, talks; silences, knit-ins, sit-ins; even marathons.	*(Still rifling, to THREE)*
VOICE 2	All held to raise funds to feed the hungry.	
VOICE 3	To help the needy, so that we can show how good and kind Christians are.	*(Standing between ONE and TWO*
VOICE 2	Then they'll be really grateful.	*(To THREE)*
VOICE 1	They'll be so grateful to us for our kindness and our true compassion that they'll all become Christian.	*(To THREE, who sits between them)*

ALL	And we'll all live happily ever after.	

ONE, TWO and THREE hold hands and sit happily.

READER 2	*(Reads Luke 4.4)*	
READER 1	*(Reads Luke 4.5-7)*	
VOICE 1	All those thousands of Jehovah's Witnesses going around from door to door?	*(Rising, to THREE)*
VOICE 3	They all seem to come to my door.	*(To ONE)*
VOICE 2	I get the Mormons.	*(To ONE)*
VOICE 1	We must learn from them; be as enthusiastic and effective,	*(To TWO and THREE)*
VOICE 2	As the gospel of double-glazing preachers, or the hot sales of the shower salesmen.	*(To ONE)*
VOICE 3	We must be deeply concerned to improve our techniques of spreading the good news.	
VOICE 1	So that we can grow at an amazing rate	*(Giving hand to TWO and the THREE)*
VOICE 2	And impress all our friends.	*(Rising with ONE's help)*
VOICE 3	And influence all our neighbouring churches	*(Rising with ONE's help as well*
VOICE 1	Showing them how alive we are.	*(All three raise their arms together)*
VOICE 2	Without, of course, ever suggesting that we think they are all as dead as dodos.	*(Laughing to other two)*
VOICE 3	·Whereas we fill all our pews.	*(Laughing)*
VOICE 2	So we must be right.	*(Laughing)*
ALL	And we'll all live happily ever after!	

ONE, TWO and THREE take hands and dance round in a circle.

READER 2	*(Reads Luke 4.8)*

TWO and THREE sit down again.

READER 1	*(Reads Luke 4.9-11)*	
VOICE 1	The Church's ancient ministry of healing has been long and sadly neglected. We have a vital role to play in reminding the world of modern, hi-tech medicine that the age of miracles is *not* past.	*(Sadly shaking head)*
VOICE 2	So we must show that *we're* able to heal too.	*(Kneeling up)*
VOICE 3	We mustn't be left out.	*(Kneeling up)*
VOICE 2	We must have healing services, laying-on-of-hands, anointing with oil, and the all-night, believing prayer meeting.	*(Kneeling up)*
VOICE 1	We must exorcize the demons which the poor, ignorant . . .	
VOICE 3	Non-Christian?	
VOICE 1	Psychiatrists and doctors call mental illness.	
VOICE 2	We must show that *we* can cure all forms of cancer with prayer, and the laying on of hands.	
VOICE 1	We must command the paraplegic to walk again.	*(Rising and holding out hands)*
VOICE 3	And if they don't, show them very kindly − for their own good − that it's because they don't have enough faith!	
VOICE 2	For their own good.	*(Rising, beckoned by ONE)*
VOICE 3	Well it's certainly not our fault if they don't respond to prayer.	*(Rising, beckoned by ONE also)*
VOICE 1	Of course not!	*(Taking THREE's arm)*
ALL	And we'll all live . . .	
VOICE 2	Well − most of us anyway.	*(Taking ONE's other arm)*
ALL	We'll all live happily for ever and ever and ever. AMEN.	

They all walk out, arm in arm.

READER 2   *(Reads Luke 4.12)*   *(Lights go out)*
READER 1   *(Reads Luke 4.13-15)*   *(The lights slowly
                                                    come back on during
                                                    reading)*

DO AS YOU WOULD BE DONE BY

A 'stand-up comic' sketch for two performers. It works best with two men, but could be played by two women or a man and a woman.

Two chairs are set downstage right and downstage left. Enter ONE from upstage right and TWO from upstage left.

VOICE 1	Hullo.	*(To TWO)*
VOICE 2	Hullo.	*(To ONE)*
VOICE 1	Hullo.	*(To audience)*
VOICE 2	Hullo.	*(To audience)*
VOICE 1	Do as you would be done by.	*(To TWO)*
VOICE 2	That's what I always say.	*(To ONE)*
VOICE 1	And Jesus said it too.	*(To TWO)*
VOICE 2	So it ought to be done . . .	*(To audience)*
VOICE 1	. . . By everyone.	*(To audience)*
VOICE 2	There was this chap, Simon Super-pants.	*(Fetching chair to left centre)*
VOICE 1	Company director.	*(Fetching chair to right centre)*
VOICE 2	Not your actual − MD!	*(Sitting left chair)*
VOICE 1	That is, for those who, unlike me, are not in tune with the jargon,	*(Sitting)*
VOICE 2	The Managing Director.	
VOICE 1	But still a big shot.	*(Rising and moving downstage)*
VOICE 2	In charge of production.	*(Rising and following)*
VOICE 1	On the factory floor.	*(Pointing downwards)*
VOICE 2	Computer wizz kid!	*(Tapping ONE on the shoulder)*
VOICE 1	Clever clogs!	*(Looking sideways at TWO)*
VOICE 2	Never wore them myself.	*(Grinning to ONE)*

VOICE 1	Simon was a clever clogs.	*(To TWO)*
VOICE 2	He worked hard himself.	*(To audience)*
VOICE 1	Expected others to do the same.	*(To audience)*
VOICE 2	Do as you would be done by.	*(In a sing-song fashion)*
VOICE 1	'Ere, that's where we came in.	*(To TWO)*
VOICE 2	So let's get on with it.	*(Impatiently to ONE)*

A very brief pause.

VOICE 1	In order to get on with it.	*(Returning to sit in right chair)*
VOICE 2	Simon read all the trade magazines.	*(Sitting in left chair)*
VOICE 1	Burned the midnight oil . . .	*(Earnestly, facing down right)*
VOICE 2	. . . And his midnight blue angle-poise lamp.	*(Earnestly, facing down left)*
VOICE 1	One day,	
VOICE 2	He read about this conference.	*(Reading from imaginary paper)*
VOICE 1	Big deal,	*(Unimpressed)*
VOICE 2	In Paris,	*(Triumphantly)*
VOICE 1	Une grande deal!	*(Exaggerated French accent)*
VOICE 2	Lasting a week.	
VOICE 1	Trés bon — une semaine!	*(Mounting excitement)*
VOICE 2	With new ideas . . .	
VOICE 1	Nouvelle idées!	
VOICE 2	. . . About increasing productivity.	
VOICE 1	Tout le . . . I give up!	

A moment's pause, as TWO glances at him then turns back to speak to audience.

VOICE 2	Got the boss . . .	
VOICE 1	Don't you mean the MD?	*(To TWO)*
VOICE 2	Sorry, the Managing Director.	*(First to ONE, then to audience)*
VOICE 1	To agree the trip.	
VOICE 2	Without the wife?	*(To ONE)*

VOICE 1	Of course − it was in Paris!	*(To TWO)*
VOICE 2	Be like taking . . .	
VOICE 2	. . . Roses to a garden centre.	

Both rise, turn their chairs to face upstage, and straddle them to talk to the audience.

VOICE 1	So off he went.
VOICE 2	All expenses paid.
VOICE 1	*All* expenses paid.
VOICE 2	But Simon Super-pants . . .
VOICE 1	. . . Went just a little bit astray.
VOICE 2	Well it *was* in Paris!
VOICE 1	Charged up several items . . .
VOICE 2	. . . Not *really* expenses . . .
VOICE 1	. . . To the firm.
VOICE 2	Little bit of this . . .
VOICE 1	. . . And rather a lot of that.
VOICE 2	Well, it *was* in Paris.

They look at one another for a moment. A slight pause.

VOICE 1	And a few months later . . .	*(Stands. Strolls over towards left chair)*
VOICE 2	There was another,	*(Stands and strolls over towards right chair)*
VOICE 1	Quite essential, productivity-producing seminar.	*(Puts right foot on chair. Looking at audience)*
VOICE 2	To which he just had to go.	*(Puts left foot on chair)*
VOICE 1	And again,	
VOICE 2	He claimed more and more,	
VOICE 1	Which he didn't really spend.	

They look at each other again.

VOICE 2	Then came the day.	*(Solemnly, taking foot from chair)*
VOICE 1	The day of reckoning. (Looking at audience)	*(Solemnly, taking foot from chair)*
VOICE 2	The day of the new auditors.	*(To audience)*

VOICE 1 & 2	Who found Simon out!	

Both collapse onto chairs.

VOICE 2	Simon Super-pants.	*(Horror-struck)*
VOICE 1	Was very, very worried.	*(Horror-struck)*
VOICE 2	Sick as a budgie!	
VOICE 1	Everyone does it!	*(Protesting to TWO)*
VOICE 2	But he'd been found out.	*(Shaking head at ONE)*
VOICE 1	Could lose his job.	*(Hushed voice)*
VOICE 2	And his golf club membership.	*(Hushed also)*
VOICE 1	Have to sell the yacht!	
VOICE 1 & 2	Worried, worried Simon.	

Both rise in panic.

VOICE 2	Saw Carruthers.	*(As ONE opens jacket)*
VOICE 1	Family GP.	*(As TWO sounds ONE's chest)*
VOICE 2	Prescribed Valium.	*(Hands over imaginary bottle)*
VOICE 1 & 2	Worried, worried Simon.	*(Both shaking heads)*

They turn chairs to face downstage and inwards.

VOICE 1	Company board meeting.	*(Sitting left chair)*
VOICE 2	Soon convened.	*(Sitting right chair)*
VOICE 1 & 2	Worried, worried Simon.	*(Both shaking heads)*
VOICE 1	Full and frank discussion.	*(Hand gestures)*
VOICE 2	Meaningful exchange of ideas.	*(Eagerly pointing finger at ONE)*
VOICE 1	To reach a unanimous decision.	*(Both lean back delighted)*
VOICE 2	Already made by the MD over his morning muesli.	*(Aside to audience)*
VOICE 1	Simon's a very good chap. Impeccable background; knew his father well. Does a first-class job. Production's better than ever.	*(In character of the MD)*
VOICE 2	Slap his wrist. Tell him to 'behave!' in future.	*(Nodding as co-director)*

VOICE 1	Simon reeled back to his office	*(Rising and walking round chair)*
VOICE 2	Couldn't believe his luck.	*(Rising and walking arond chair)*
VOICE 1 & 2	Happy, happy Simon.	*(Waving arms with delight)*
VOICE 1	He'd been let off the hook.	*(They embrace euphorically)*
VOICE 1 & 2	Happy, happy Simon.	*(Both sit down again)*
VOICE 2	Hello, lovely house!	*(Waving to house)*
VOICE 1	Hello, lovely Golf Club!	*(Waving to Golf Club)*
VOICE 2	Hello, lovely yacht!	*(Waving to yacht)*
VOICE 1	Hello, everybody!	*(Waving to audience)*
VOICE 2	Hello, what's this?	*(Suddenly angry)*
VOICE 1	Asked Simon.	*(To audience)*
VOICE 2	Where's Miss Potter?	*(Angrily to ONE)*
VOICE 1	My little secretary.	*(Angrily to TWO)*
VOICE 2	She should be here.	
VOICE 1	I want to dictate some new directives with renewed enthusiasm and gratitude for being safe in my job again.	
VOICE 2	Where's Miss Potter?	*(Louder)*
VOICE 1	I want to work forever! Where's Miss Potter?	*(Louder still)*
VOICE 2	'Scuse me, sir.	*(Standing up, tea-lady's voice)*
VOICE 1	Said the tea-lady.	*(Standing up, to audience)*
VOICE 2	Yes? snapped Simon.	*(Sitting down again)*
VOICE 1	Miss Potter said that her mother is very ill. You know how she looks after her, well she's gone down the chemist to get the prescription. The doctor said her mother should have the medicine as soon as possible, and Miss Potter didn't think you'd be finished so soon. She'll be back in a minute, I'm sure.	*(Very fast in tea-lady's voice)*

VOICE 2	She needn't bother.	*(Grimly to ONE)*
VOICE 1	Said Simon.	*(To audience)*
VOICE 2	If we are to maintain production, we cannot allow this kind of thing to go on.	*(Rising, pompously to ONE)*
VOICE 1	Miss Potter is sacked.	*(To audience)*
VOICE 2	Forthwith.	*(To audience)*
VOICE 1	At once.	
VOICE 2	Immediately.	

Pause.

VOICE 1	Do as you would be done by.	*(In a sing-song voice to TWO)*
VOICE 2	That's what I . . .	*(To ONE)*

ONE's voice dies away as they both become embarrassed. They each clap a hand over their mouth, turn and exit hurriedly in opposite directions.

A PARABLE FOR TODAY

A 'stand-up comic' sketch for two performers of either sex.

There is a bench centre stage. Enter ONE from upstage right and TWO from upstage left.

VOICE 1	Hello!	*(Moving towards TWO)*
VOICE 2	Good morning!	*(Moving to meet ONE below bench)*
VOICE 1	How do you know?	*(To TWO)*
VOICE 2	Know what?	*(To ONE)*
VOICE 1	That it's a good morning?	
VOICE 2	I dunno.	
VOICE 1	So what is a good morning?	
VOICE 2	What is a good day?	
VOICE 1	What is a good life?	
VOICE 2	Here's a story Jesus told.	*(To audience step downstage)*
VOICE 1	Featuring Felicity Kendal and Richard . . .	*(To audience step downstage)*
VOICE 2	No! No!	*(To ONE)*
VOICE 1	Not that good life!	*(To TWO)*
VOICE 2	No, about a different sort of good life!	
VOICE 1	Good.	
VOICE 2	So let's get on with it.	*(Impatiently)*
VOICE 1	That's Good.	
VOICE 2	There was this chap.	*(Another step down to audience)*
VOICE 1	Good show!	
VOICE 2	Oh, for goodness sake, let's get on with it!	*(Irritably to ONE)*
VOICE 1	Good idea!	*(Cheerfully to TWO)*

VOICE 2	Good grief!	*(Desperately to audience)*
VOICE 1	So there was this chap.	
VOICE 2	That's right — so you said. A very good sort.	*(Ignoring ONE)*
VOICE 1	Came from a good home.	*(To audience)*
VOICE 2	Not to say an impeccable background.	*(To audience in a public school accent)*
VOICE 1	Father had an awfully good job.	
VOICE 2	Something big in the City.	*(Trying to remember)*
VOICE 1	Merchant bank or something.	*(Trying to remember)*
VOICE 2	Mother was a good sort . . .	*(Another step downstage)*
VOICE 1	Did a good job.	*(Another step downstage)*
VOICE 2	Brought up the children.	*(Moving slightly stage left)*
VOICE 1	Boy and a girl.	*(Moving slightly stage right)*
VOICE 2	Taught them good manners.	*(Smiling)*
VOICE 1	Gave them good standards.	*(Nodding)*
VOICE 2	Chose good schools for them.	*(New thought)*
VOICE 1	Winchester for the boy,	*(Smiling)*
VOICE 2	St Gertrude's for the girl.	*(Smiling)*
VOICE 1	St Who's?	*(Startled, to TWO)*
VOICE 2	Well, it's good enough for a girl.	*(To ONE with a shrug)*
VOICE 1	All she needs is enough education to be a good wife and mother.	*(Sagely, nodding agreement)*
VOICE 2	But he needs to get on in the world.	*(To ONE)*
VOICE 1	And for that, he needs a good start.	
VOICE 2	Father gave him that.	*(Moving to the left of bench)*
VOICE 1	After university,	*(Moving to right of bench)*
VOICE 2	Set the boy up in business.	*(To audience)*
VOICE 1	In just a small way.	*(To audience)*

VOICE 2	With an office and half a secretary.	(Winking to audience)
VOICE 1	Acted as a broker.	
VOICE 2	Buying and selling.	
VOICE 1	What?	(Stopping suddenly, to TWO)
VOICE 2	Anything he could get a good price for.	(Carelessly, to ONE)
VOICE 1	He was a good salesman.	(To audience)
VOICE 2	He did real good.	(To audience)
VOICE 1	He soon had a big office.	(Stands on bench)
VOICE 2	With five and a half secretaries, six computers, five word processors, two fax machines . . .	(Stands on bench)
VOICE 1	Soon got a good amount of capital.	
VOICE 2	Bought up a firm of estate agents.	
VOICE 1	With a good deal of good property on its books, and a good reputation to book.	(With hand on TWO's shoulder)
VOICE 2	Had to pay a lot for the goodwill.	
VOICE 1	But he made a go of it.	(Smiling at TWO)
VOICE 2	Kept the good staff.	(Smiling)
VOICE 1	Moved out the not-so-good ones.	(Winking at TWO)
VOICE 2	Brought in good ideas.	(Nodding at ONE)
VOICE 1	Sound − not flashy!	(Gravely agreeing)
VOICE 2	Bought himself a good house in a good neighbourhood.	(To audience, admiringly)
VOICE 1	Married a very nice girl − good as gold, she was.	(Smiling to audience)
VOICE 2	Gave him good food, good support.	
VOICE 1	Good-looking as well.	(Nudging ONE)
VOICE 2	Sounds too good to be true!	(Raising eyebrows to TWO)
VOICE 1	She turned out to have a good eye	(To audience)

VOICE 2	For bargains — genuine antiques at very low prices.	*(To audience)*
VOICE 1	In church jumble sales, and charity shops.	
VOICE 2	Made a very good living for herself . . .	
VOICE 1	. . . In addition to her husband's business.	
VOICE 2	So they bought themselves an even bigger house.	*(Coming down from bench)*
VOICE 1	A lovely old manor with several acres of paddock attached.	*(Coming down from bench)*
VOICE 2	Used to have lovely parties . . .	*(Coming downstage centre)*
VOICE 1	. . . In their beautiful house full of beautiful things.	
VOICE 2	Not to mention two beautiful children.	
VOICE 1	It truly was — the good life.	
VOICE 2	He decided to retire early.	
VOICE 1	To enjoy all these good things properly.	
VOICE 2	What a good idea!	*(To ONE)*
VOICE 1	Everyone said.	*(To audience)*
VOICE 2	Had a farewell party . . .	*(Going up to bench)*
VOICE 1	. . . At the office.	*(Going up to bench)*
VOICE 2	Everyone had a really good time.	*(Enjoying themselves)*
VOICE 1	Driving home.	*(Both sitting on bench)*
VOICE 2	A good-for-nothing kid, in a crummy old banger.	
VOICE 1	Swerved right in front of him.	*(Miming swerve)*
VOICE 2	He swerved as well,	*(Miming swerve)*
VOICE 1	. . . Straight into a wall!	*(Both scream)*
VOICE 2	Died instantly.	*(Both stand up)*
VOICE 1	Terrible tragedy.	*(Both bow heads)*
VOICE 2	What a waste!	*(To ONE)*
VOICE 1	It makes you ask questions,	*(To TWO)*
VOICE 2	A man like that . . . never did anyone any harm. He lived a good life — why did he have to	*(Going downstage to audience)*

	die like that?	
VOICE 1	Good question.	*(Coming to join ONE)*
VOICE 2	But Jesus asks another question.	*(To audience)*
VOICE 1	What's that?	*(To TWO)*
VOICE 2	What did he live for?	

There is a pause, while they look at each other, then speak to the audience.

VOICE 1 & 2 Very good question!

They link arms and exit.

THE WATCHFUL SERVANTS

A sketch intended for four men, but with very slight changes of text it can work equally well for four women, but do not mix sexes.

Unlike the previous three sketches, this is not addressed to the audience, but a one act play in the manner of the 'Theatre of the Absurd' - delivering the surrealistic lines naturally.

TWO, THREE and FOUR are seated on three chairs in a semicircle at stage right, reading newspapers. Enter ONE, very excited carrying a letter. He grabs the back of a chair stage left. TWO and FOUR disappear behind their newspapers when they are not speaking.

VOICE 1	*(Excited and happy)* Good morning!
VOICE 2	*(Slightly lowering paper, surprised, to ONE)* Pardon?
VOICE 3	*(Putting paper down instead)* He said, good morning.
VOICE 4	*(Slightly lowering paper, shocked, to THREE)* Did he?
VOICE 3	*(To FOUR)* Yes, he did.
VOICE 2	*(Who has not heard the last two remarks)* Did what?
VOICE 1	I said good morning.
VOICE 4	*(Losing interest)* Oh. *(Disappears behind paper)*
VOICE 3	*(To FOUR)* You don't sound very interested.
VOICE 2	*(Bewildered to THREE)* Interested in what?
VOICE 1	In a good morning.
VOICE 4	*(Wearily laying down paper)* But everybody says, good morning.
VOICE 2	*(Patiently)* When you get into work everyone says good morning.
VOICE 4	*(Driving it home)* At home, when we get up, we say good morning.
VOICE 2	Everyone says good morning.
VOICE 4	Every day, everyone says to everyone else, good morning.
VOICE 1	*(Pausing slightly)* Not on the tube they don't!
VOICE 3	*(Getting interested)* That's different, that's not real life.
VOICE 1	If they did speak on the tube, you would notice that!
VOICE 2	*(Trying to make ONE understand)* But we're not on the tube

	so why should we notice when people say good morning?
VOICE 3	*(Thinking it over)* Do they all say it the same way?
VOICE 4	*(Uninterested)* More or less.
VOICE 1	Doesn't it sound different from different people?
VOICE 3	Like - good morning. *(Trying various ways of saying it: eg bright, gloomy, whispered, loud etc)*
VOICE 2	But it's still saying the same thing isn't it?
VOICE 1	But the way it's said says something about the person concerned. It says that they're happy, or miserable, relieved, or struggling, frightened, lonely.
VOICE 4	*(Irritably)* So what?
VOICE 1	*(Explaining)* So we can hear something about the kind of person they are.
VOICE 3	*(Explaining)* So we can hear what kind of things have been happening to them.
VOICE 1	And if it's been something good we can enjoy it with them.
VOICE 3	And it might cheer us up as well.
VOICE 1	If you listen carefully, you might hear something important.
VOICE 3	But if you don't listen properly you might miss the most important thing.
VOICE 2	*(Arguing back)* But if you listen, you might hear that something terrible has happened to them.
VOICE 4	*(Agreeing with TWO)* And then we might have to listen to their troubles.
VOICE 2	And that could make us miserable as well.
VOICE 2 & 4	*(Triumphantly)* And we might have to do something about it.

TWO and FOUR return behind their newspapers. A pause. When the conversation resumes, TWO and FOUR are even more crusty, in the style of old people complaining about the younger generation.

VOICE 1	*(Needling TWO and FOUR gently)* So you don't listen.
VOICE 3	*(Following ONE's example)* In case you get involved.
VOICE 4	*(Stone-walling)* That's what we don't want.
VOICE 2	*(Stone-walling as well)* To get involved.
VOICE 1	So, all right, you don't want to get involved. All I said was good morning.
VOICE 2	We know. *(Goes back to the paper)*
VOICE 4	We know. *(Returns to his paper)*
VOICE 1	You didn't notice anything different about it?

VOICE 2	*(Getting annoyed)* We haven't got time to notice differences.
VOICE 4	*(Getting annoyed)* We didn't get where we are today by noticing differences.
VOICE 2	Got to stick to the everyday routine.
VOICE 4	Nose to the grindstone.
VOICE 2	Shoulder to the wheel.
VOICE 4	Never mind looking at the wood - just see the trees.
VOICE 2	When I was a lad we didn't have time to go about in a day-dream, looking for differences. We couldn't afford differences.

> *TWO and FOUR return to their papers and lose interest in what ONE and THREE are saying.*

VOICE 1	But you don't see the trees or the wood. Your eyes are closed. I think it's a great morning.
VOICE 3	*(To ONE)* You sound very exceptionally bright this morning. Is it *that* good a morning?
VOICE 1	It sure is. I've just heard that I've won a prize - a holiday for two in the Bahamas. *(Addressing THREE)* Will you come with me?
	TWO and FOUR look up with a start
VOICE 3	*(Jumping up to join ONE)* You bet! I'd love to!
VOICE 2	*(Standing up hurt)* What about me?
VOICE 4	*(Also standing up hurt)* What about me?
VOICE 1	*(Smiling)* Oh, you don't want to get involved.
VOICE 1 & 3	*(Gently)* Good morning.

> *Exit ONE and THREE stage left. TWO and FOUR look at each other in dismay. They exit right.*

THE GOOD SAMARITAN

A sketch for three performers of either sex. This is another sketch in the manner the 'Theatre of the Absurd' and it should therefore be played 'straight'. The text can be adapted as necessary where appropriate.

ONE, TWO and THREE are sitting on bar stools holding mugs or glasses. During the scene they can drink and gesture freely, but they must all have finished drinking by the end.

It is important in this scene that TWO should never guess the significance of what he is saying.

VOICE 1	*(Shrugging)* I mean to say, I ask you.
VOICE 2	*(Puzzled)* What?
VOICE 3	*(Explaining)* It's just not sensible.
VOICE 1	*(Shaking head)* Everyone knows how dangerous it is down there. Wilderness Road is a paradise for thieves.
VOICE 2	*(Surprised)* Really.
VOICE 3	*(Nodding)* Robbers, hooligans, vandals . . .
VOICE 1	Go down there on your own and you're asking for trouble.
VOICE 2	*(Amazed)* You aren't saying that he *asked* to be mugged are you?
VOICE 3	What we're *saying* is that no one with any sense at all goes down that road on their own.
VOICE 2	*(Objecting rather feebly)* Maybe some people have to go down there to live or work.
VOICE 3	*(Shaking head)* It makes no difference who they are or why they're there. Daylight robbery or midnight murder - you get it all along that road.
VOICE 1	*(Thoughtfully)* Serves him right, in a way.
VOICE 2	*(Amazed)* You mean he asked to be robbed, beaten up and mugged?
VOICE 3	*(Raising a finger)* Got it exactly. No decent person goes down there. Not if he has any sense!
VOICE 1	*(Continuing the story)* Anyway those yobbos knocked him

	senseless. Serve him right if he had been left there.
VOICE 2	*(Distressed)* Lying in the gutter.
VOICE 3	*(Nodding)* 'Til he came to his senses.
VOICE 1	*(Nodding)* Maybe he'd have learned a lesson.
VOICE 2	*(Puzzled)* That being mugged is horrible?
VOICE 3	*(With satisfaction)* And he got the message alright.
VOICE 2	The vicar gave us the message.
VOICE 1	*(Catching THREE's drift)* The vicar?
VOICE 3	Yes, he told us about it at the evening service.
VOICE 1	He said he'd seen the man lying in the gutter, covered in blood, when he drove past him on the way to the early morning service.
VOICE 3	He knew he was drunk of course.
VOICE 2	*(Thoroughly muddled)* Who, the vicar?
VOICE 1	*(Amused)* No, the man in the gutter. He told us that he'd been reading a book about alcoholics and could recognise all the signs.
VOICE 2	*(Trying to follow)* The man in the gutter had been reading a book?
VOICE 3	*(Patiently)* No! The vicar had. Well-read man, is the vicar, and he knows his Bible. He helps you to make sense of things. He compared it all to the story of the Good Samaritan.
VOICE 2	*(Innocently)* How did he do that?
VOICE 1	Well, he told us that, as he drove past again on his way home, the man was still there. All those people passing by on the other side. None of them showing any sign of loving their neighbour.
VOICE 3	*(Gravely)* Terrible indictment of our society. People just don't care any more. As the vicar says, the only *Neighbours* they love - are the ones on the telly. *(They all smile or nod agreement - whichever is in character)*. All those passers-by just left the man there.
VOICE 2	How could you be sure it was the same man lying there?
VOICE 1	The church-warden said he'd seen him too. Described him exactly, and we all know what a solid, sensible chap he is . . .
VOICE 2	When did he see him?
VOICE 3	Around the same time.
VOICE 1	He was afraid to stop because he didn't want to end up in the same state.
VOICE 3	*(Nodding)* Very sensible.
VOICE 2	*(Just asking)* So they both just left him there?
VOICE 3	*(Indignantly)* No! Of course not.

VOICE 1	*(High moral line)* The church-warden rang the local paper and the local radio station to complain about the lawlessness of society today and how it's no longer safe to walk the streets.
VOICE 3	*(High moral line)* Good for him, very-public spirited that. And what were they going to do about it?
VOICE 2	What happened to the man in the gutter?
VOICE 1	Well, after the church-warden had made his point perfectly clear to the local media, he rang for an ambulance and told the police.
VOICE 3	But they told him that the man had already been take to casualty at Jericho Hospital.
VOICE 2	*(Surprised)* Really?
VOICE 1	*(With distaste)* Seems some fellow, Iraqi or something they said, had seen him lying there and picked him up, put him in his car and taken him off to the Jericho.
VOICE 3	*(Also with distaste)* Then he went to the man's wife and family, and took them to the hospital.
VOICE 2	*(Innocently)* Good thing there are people like that about.
VOICE 1	*(Suspiciously, getting down from the stool)* Makes you wonder how he happened to be on the spot.
VOICE 3	*(Getting down as well)* Yes. An Iraqi? - doesn't sound right, does it? Bit suspicious, that. Doesn't make sense to me.
VOICE 1	*(Knowledgeably)* He's a Muslim, what would he know about loving your neighbour?
VOICE 2	*(Getting the point at last)* You mean only Christians love their neighbour?
VOICE 1 & 3	Of course! It's in the Bible, isn't it?
VOICE 2	*(A sudden thought)* But it's in the Old Testament first. It's a Jewish commandment.
VOICE 1	*(Sternly)* Don't go confusing the issue like that.
VOICE 3	*(Light dawning)* I think I see it now. I read somewhere that many Iraqis are Christians.
VOICE 1	*(Relieved)* So that's why he helped the traveller. He would know about loving your neighbour, being a Christian!
VOICE 3	That makes sense now.

Pause while they all finish their drinks.

VOICE 2	*(Still a little confused)* Does it?

ONE and THREE look at TWO and shake their heads disapprovingly, then exit left. Exit TWO right, still puzzled.

THE LOST COIN

A sketch for two performers, ideally ONE should be played by a woman and TWO a man. There is also a NARRATOR who speaks one line near the end, possibly from a lectern.

There is a table stage right with an upright chair beside it, and a lounge chair stage left. TWO sits in the lounge chair, doing a crossword puzzle. Enter ONE, stage right, wearing an apron and holding a duster.

VOICE 1	*(Worried)* Where is it?
VOICE 2	*(Not looking up)* Where's what?
VOICE 1	*(Struggling to find word)* You know the urgh . . .
VOICE 2	I don't.
VOICE 1	The wotsit.
VOICE 2	*(Looking up puzzled)* Wotsit?
VOICE 1	*(Impatiently)* You *know*.
VOICE 2	I *don't*.
VOICE 1	The thingy.
VOICE 2	What thingy?
VOICE 1	You know.
VOICE 2	I don't.
VOICE 1	*(Desperately)* The wotsit, the thingy.
VOICE 2	*(Giving up)* I have a funny feeling that this could go on for a very long time. *(Goes back to crossword)*
VOICE 1	*(Going to him and shaking duster)* Well, it will if you don't help me find it.
VOICE 2	*(Looking up, irritably)* Find what?
VOICE 1	What I've lost.
VOICE 2	What shall I take, tranquillisers, cyanide, or the ferry to Boulogne?
VOICE 1	Take what you like, as long as I find it.
VOICE 2	Is it that important? *(Turns back to crossword)*
VOICE 1	Of course, something's missing in my life without it.

VOICE 2	*(Without looking up)* I know someone who has got something missing.
VOICE 1	*(Suddenly remembering the word)* That's right, there's a cup missing.
VOICE 2	*(Surprised, putting paper down)* I don't think I can be hearing this right.
VOICE 1	Has your hearing gone funny? Lost your hearing aid?
VOICE 2	I didn't think I needed one, but I could have sworn just now that you said you had lost a cup.
VOICE 1	I did.
VOICE 2	*(Sitting up straight)* All this flapdoodle, tarradiddle, panic and hysterics has been over a cup?
VOICE 1	Yes.
VOICE 2	*(Sarcastically)* The FA Cup, Cheltenham Gold Cup, World Cup, Waterloo Cup?
VOICE 1	No! Just a teacup.
VOICE 2	A special teacup? One filled to its tiny brim with sentimental memories; last drunk out of by the Queen, Terry Wogan, or that ginger tom down the road?
VOICE 1	No. Just an ordinary teacup - from that set we got in the sales six years ago.
VOICE 2	But there's a dozen cups in that set. We never use a dozen teacups.
VOICE 1	Well, I can only find eleven now.
VOICE 2	*(Swinging arm on leg of chair)* Maybe it has been washed away by a million afternoon teas; dissolved in washing-up liquid or been stolen by extra-terrestrial, teacup-obsessed aliens searching for the meaning of life.
VOICE 1	*(Wanting to hit him)* Why can't you be serious?
VOICE 2	*(Mock serious)* Perhaps it has been spirited away to a remote tribal village where savages worship it as a sign of a distant deity.
VOICE 1	*(Flicking duster at him)* Oh, stop it, be serious!
VOICE 2	*(Thinking hard)* Maybe, it has gone to a retirement home for distressed and elderly crockery.
VOICE 1	*(Shouting at him)* Please be serious!
VOICE 2	*(Kneeling in his chair with mock devotion)* Or perhaps it's earthly course being run, of providing the beverage that cheers but not inebriates, it has gone to the great teacup home in the sky. *(He is enjoying this)*
VOICE 1	*(Deadly quiet)* Be serious.

VOICE 2	*(Coming off it)* I *am* being serious. I'm wondering why on earth you are making all this fuss about one very ordinary little teacup, when we've got eleven more in the same set, and I don't know how many others stored away.
VOICE 1	*(Accusingly)* Of course, you wouldn't know, you never dust the crockery cupboard. You wouldn't know how many cups we've got.
VOICE 2	*(Challenging her)* Do you?
VOICE 1	*(Stumped)* No . . . but I know there's one missing.
VOICE 2	*(Sitting back in chair)* Don't start that again, I can't take any more.
VOICE 1	I bet you could take a cup of tea though, couldn't you?
VOICE 2	*(Sighing)* I think I need one, after all this excitement. My nerves are like a used tea-bag.
VOICE 1	*(With patient irony)* Well then, you know where the teapot is, and the tea, and the milk and the sugar, and if you think very hard you might even be able to find your way to the kitchen.
VOICE 2	*(Stands up to go, then turns back to her)* Where are the teacups?
VOICE 1	Be serious!

TWO exits stage right. While he is gone, ONE wanders round staring in all directions.

VOICE 1	*(To herself)* Where is it? Where can it have got to? Oh, where has the stupid thing gone?

Despairingly she throws herself down in the lounge chair. Enter TWO, carrying a tea-tray with the tea things and two teacups.

VOICE 2	*(Putting tray on table)* Here we are. Tea for two. I kept my finger on both of the teacups in case one was spirited away on the long and hazardous journey from the kitchen, and the even longer one from the bottom of the garden.
VOICE 1	*(Sitting up in the chair)* This may sound a silly question, but why did you have to go to the bottom of the garden to make the tea? Have you got a tea-plantation down there? Or a cow for the milk?
VOICE 2	*(Pouring the tea)* No. But as I was waiting for the kettle to boil I remembered that last summer I took a teacup to my tool shed and I wondered if it was still there and, if it was . . . *(Pulling a third cup from pocket)*

VOICE 1   *(Jumping up and rushing to cup)* *It is! It is!* You've found it. You're forgiven for everything. You've found my missing teacup. Hallelujah! Let's celebrate! Let's open a new packet of biscuits.

VOICE 2   Steady on. Don't let's go overboard about finding one little cup. One cup can't matter that much. You cannot be serious!

NARRATOR   Every coin that is lost, every sheep that is lost, every person that is alive, matters supremely to God. *(ONE and TWO listen intently)*

VOICE 1   *(To TWO)* That's right, that's what the wotsit says.

VOICE 2   *(To ONE)* You mean the thingy.

> *They both look away from one another, straining to think of the word. Suddenly it comes to them, and they turn to each other.*

VOICE 1 & 2   The Bible?

A WEALTH OF RESOURCES FROM NCEC

WHAT A GOOD IDEA!

NOTES On Bible Reading

Fergus Travels South

The Story of JESUS

TURN BUT A STONE
Edmund B.

Spectrum
An inter-church training programme for youth workers

RAINBOW

Think Again
by Linda

NATIONAL CHRISTIAN EDUCATION COUNCIL

NCEC

CATALOGUE

Hillside Publishing
IBRA
International Bible Reading Association

TRAINING

BIBLE STUDY

SUPPLIES

ASSEMBLY IDEAS

MUSIC

PLAYS

STORIES

GROUP DISCUSSION

NCEC

Other Titles from RADIUS and NCEC

THE HILL
Sylvia Read
0-7197-0761-7

A modern mystery play in which the characters find themselves caught up in the experience of Easter. 30 mins.

Code No. PLA0761 (A)

CROSSTALK
Bob Irving
0-7197-0795-1

A collection of ten short plays based upon the parables which were, in their own time, sharp contemporary stories in an established tradition. In order to convey the same sense of immediacy these sketches are presented in a highly modern quick-firing style. No need for props or costumes, maximum cast of five. Each play lasts about 5 minutes.

Code No. PLA0795 (A)

SURPRISE SKETCHES
Ronald Rich
0-7197-0796-X

Five one-act plays with surprising endings. Ideal as a prompter for discussion or for use in worship, these plays examine some familiar human failings in a new stimulating style. Each play runs for about 10 minutes.

Code No. PLA0796 (A)

THE FLAME
Edmund Banyard
0-7197-0709-9

A novel approach to the idea of Pentecost, this play is a one act fantasy in the style of the Theatre of the Absurd. Four ordinary people are offered the 'Light of the World' by a messenger from the border between Time and Eternity. 25 mins.

Code No. FLA0709 (A)

Performance times given are
very approximate.

A FISTFUL OF FIVERS
Edmund Banyard
0-7197-0667-X

Twelve five-minute plays, each with a Christian message. Using the minimum of actors, scenery and props, these lively sketches will appeal to everyone who is young in the widest sense.

Code No. PLA0667 (A)

A FUNNY THING HAPPENED ON THE WAY TO JERICHO
Tom Long
0-7197-0722-6

The dress rehearsal for a presentation of the Good Samaritan turns out to be more than the leading player intended, as she is challenged by each of the roles she takes on in her search for the one she feels happy with. 30 mins.

Code No. FUN0722 (A) R

THE PRODIGAL DAUGHTER
William Fry
0-7197-0668-8

Using a neat twist, William Fry has turned one of the best-known parables into the tale of a present-day girl, updating the setting to portray some of the concerns of modern society. While it shows the seamier side of contemporary life, the message of this play is ultimately one of redemption and love. 30 mins.

Code No. PLA0668 (A)

NATIVITY LETTERS
Nick Warburton
0-7197-0724-2

Highlights the strains put on mother and daughter in the interdependence of a single parent family, which make them tend to disassociate themselves from other people. Help eventually presents itself through a committed teacher in the daughter's drama group. 40 mins.

Code No. NAT0724 (A)

WHO'LL BE BROTHER DONKEY?
Arthur Scholey
0-7197-0723-4

Three traditional Christmas tales are combined to produce this play where the animals use their Christmas Eve gift of speech to enact the crib scene in the hillside chapel. During the journey from their stable they outwit the wily Fox and Vixen in their malevolent schemes. The conclusion shows how the preparation of the crib scene is achieved against all odds through forgiveness of their fellow creatures and faith. 60 mins.

Code No. WHO0723 (A)